Terqa Preliminary Reports, No. 8:
OBJECT TYPOLOGY OF THE THIRD SEASON: THE THIRD AND SECOND MILLENNIA

by
Linda Mount-Williams*

A typological analysis of 96 objects found during the third season (September-December 1977). These objects, dating to the third and second millennia, include clay figurines, metal pins, weapons and tools, beads, rings and miscellaneous implements. A descriptive catalog provides a detailed entry for each item, with cross references to the Object Typology of the Second Season (*TPR* 3). Most objects are also illustrated in line drawings and half-tones.

Table of Contents

*   The author wishes to thank Senior Museum Scientist LouElla Saul of the University of California for the shell identifications. The drawings are by Linda Mount·Williams and Samir Toueir, and the photographs by Brenda Sokolowski and Linda Mount-Williams. This excavation is made possible by grants from the Ambassador International Cultural Foundation and the S. H. Kress Foundation.

1. Introduction

During the third season at Terqa (September-December 1977) numerous objects of various types dating from the Islamic period to the middle of the third millennium B.C. were excavated. The objects recovered from the second and third millennia are arranged in the catalog according to typological criteria.

One category of objects, the stone material, is not presented. These artifacts will be discussed with the stone objects from the second season in a later fascicle. The Islamic objects and pottery of the third season will also be discussed in a separate fascicle (see TPR 5 for the Islamic objects from the second season).

2. Typological Analysis

2.1 Ostrich egg, pottery stand and inlaid rim

One ostrich egg was found in Area B (see TPR 6, Fig. 1 for area location). It was excavated near the skull of the adult, female burial in SG14. The burial, containing a total of twelve vessels, numerous gypsum beads, an ostrich egg, two globular headed pins, a bronze ring, an inlaid bead, two rhomboid beads, a bead container, and two shells, dated to the third millennium (Fig. 1; Ill. 1 and 2). She was buried on her left side, in a flexed position, her arms embracing a vessel (TPR 9 47). Within the vessel were two rhomboid beads, a bronze ring, and an inlaid bead (TPR 8 23, 63, 64 and 79). Across the vessel were the two globular headed pins. The gypsum beads were sprinkled around her hips, back and head.

A conical ceramic stand and fragmented ceramic rim inlaid with triangular pieces of mother-of-pearl were excavated adjacent to the egg. Bitumen was used to adhere the pieces to the ceramic. The egg had been sliced approximately one quarter of the way down and the rim adhered to it (see reconstruction Fig. 3). The egg surface was probably painted in a linear design. It is, however, possible that the egg was bound with some material which left a pattern on the surface.

Parallels for this type of triangular mosaic work on ostrich shells and the addition of a ceramic rim and base can be found at Ur in Shub-ad's tomb and other burials, Kish in grave 2, and Mari in the Ishtar Temple, level b. The ostrich eggs, used as cups, frequently have shell incrusted rims with a bitumen base; they are usually sliced about one quarter of the way down, and are often decorated with triangular pieces of mother-of-pearl (Parrot, 1956, Pl. LXXI:a). Some may have been dipped in red paint (Woolley, 1934, Pg. 132). At Ur, a copy of an ostrich egg in gold, with a base and rim of applied mosaic in lapis-lazuli, red limestone, and mother-of-pearl, was uncovered. Another example, similar to the egg uncovered in Area B, is an ostrich shell vase to which a clay foot and clay mouth was attached. The mouth has a flat rim decorated with incrustation of red paste and mother-of-pearl (Woolley, 1934, Pg. 166). The ostrich egg cup from Shub-ad's tomb at Ur was incrusted around the rim and base with mother-of-pearl inlay set in bitumen. Ostrich egg fragments from the mid-second millennium have also been uncovered at Nuzi. These were, however, undecorated and too fragmented to reconstruct. At Terqa, a bitumen object was

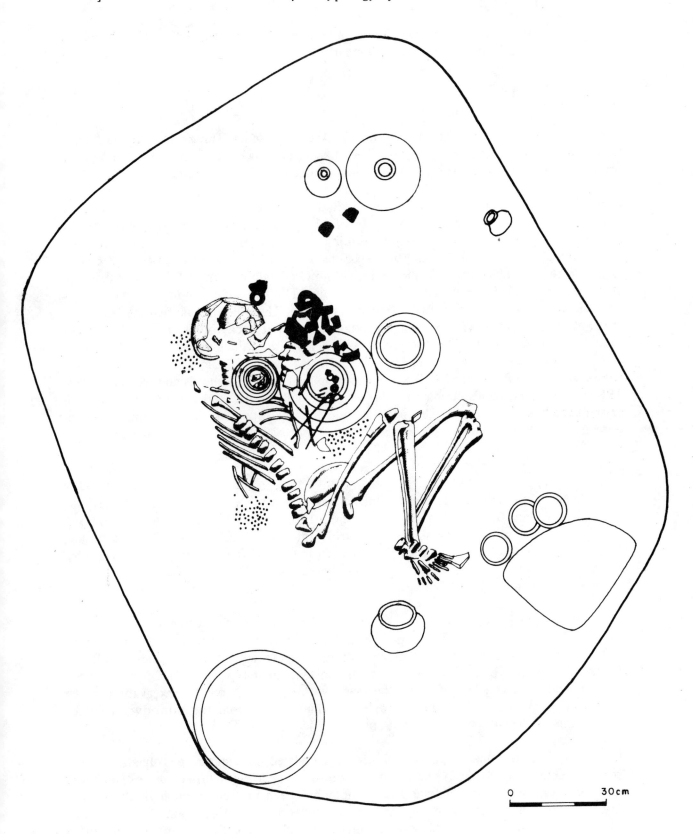

Figure 1. Third millennium shaft grave showing placement of objects (shell disc and bead container near forehead; pins; beads and metal ring on vessel; ostrich egg fragments, rim, and base; scattered gypsum beads; shells).

uncovered in the 1924 excavation (Thureau-Dangin and Dhorme, 1924, Pl. LX fig. 1), incrusted with small triangles of mother-of-pearl.

2.2 Figurines

Several clay figurine fragments were found this season at Terqa. Three represent the typical handmade, crude females, one shows a robed male of which only the trunk and legs are preserved, and four represent moldmade females, none of which are complete.

One of the three crude female figurines, TPR 8 4, has a beaked nose, round pellet eyes with stabs representing pupils, and traces of black paint surrounding the eyes. Across the forehead are parallel incisions representing hair while around the front of her neck is an applied necklace filled with short, parallel slashes. The second fragment, TPR 8 5, is the torso of a female with a pinched waist, incised pubic triangle filled with diagonal stabs, and pronounced buttocks. The last female, TPR 8 6, is a crude, schematic torso with an applied pellet pendant filled with punctations. The other female figurine fragments are moldmade plaques with bodies projecting from a flat background: TPR 8 7 has well-modeled, rounded thighs; TPR 8 8 has well modeled hips, a shallow depression for a navel, and rounded, tapering legs. Two poorly preserved moldmade female heads were also recovered. Both TPR 8 9 and TPR 8 10 are stylized with wide foreheads and narrow cheeks. TPR 8 9 has both hands cupping her breasts, hair pulled back, and two incised lines indicating bracelets on her arms. This is a common figurine type of second millennium Mesopotamia. TPR 8 10 is also moldmade with bangs and thick locks or plaits hanging on each side of her face.

The female torso, TPR 8 11, is a moldmade fragment broken at the neck and knees. She is wearing a long, fitted, "V"-necked dress held to each side by her hands to reveal her nudity. The well preserved plaque representing the male figurine, TRP 8 12, is broken below the waist and at the ankles. He wears an ankle-length wrap around style tasseled robe, with the fringed end draped over his shoulder (this is a very common male dress in second millennium Mesopotamia).

Parallels for the female head with necklace can be found at Tell Chuēra, Chagar Bazar, Mari, Selenkahiye, Harran, Tello, and Ur and date from the mid-third and early second millennia B.C. Parallels for the handmade female figure with incised pubic triangle can be found at Mari where they are among the most frequent type of female figurine. Analogies to the Terqa male plaque can be made with figurines from the excavations at Ur and Mari (small statue of Idi-Lum and Ishtup Ilum dating from the third dynasty of Ur to the nineteenth century, Parrot, 1959, pgs. 18-21).

In addition to the human figurines, three hand-modeled, schematic quadrupeds were uncovered. One, TPR 8 13, is the typical, crude quadruped with broken horns, tail, four tapering legs, and broad hindquarters. A hole has been pierced through the head. Van Loon suggests that such holes may have been used for reins (Van Loon, 1968, pg. 29). The other example, TPR 8 14, is a schematic animal head with two stubby ears and a short, pointed snout. A round central perforation through the long axis seems to indicate that it was used as a spout. The last example, TPR 8 15, is a cloven hoof with two incised lines delineating the hoof and a deep central groove splitting the hoof in half.

2.3 Metal Objects

Many metal objects including weapons, tools, and jewelry came from all areas of the excavation, as well as those given to the excavation by local inhabitants. The weapons include an axe, leaf-shaped daggar, and tanged arrowhead; the tool category contains a saw* and tweezers; jewelry includes pins, rings, and earrings. In addition to these implements, several fragments of bronze were too corroded to identify. The bronze implements referred to in this fascicle have not yet been analyzed.

Two poorly preserved pin fragments come from SG 7. TPR 8 17 is bent and rounded in cross-section. One loop-headed or spiral headed pin, TPR 8 18, was excavated in a firepit of SG 10, level 6. It is rectangular in cross-section and tapers to a point. Similar pins have been excavated at Ur, Mari, Til-Barsib, Kish, and Tepe Gawra. This pin type seems to have been manufactured during the Early Dynastic III period and continues into the second millennium.

Two pins, TPR 8 19 and 20, were found resting on vessel TPR 9 47 of the female burial 1 of SG 14. Both are identical, perforated, globular-headed pins, bent near the globe. The shanks are long and taper to a point. These pins were associated with two conoid beads, a small gypsum bead with flecks of quartz (?) inlay, and a bronze (?) ring (see reconstruction Fig. 2). It seems that they were worn as is illustrated on a frieze from Mari dating to the Early Dynastic III period (Parrot, 1962, Pl. XI: 2, 3, and 4 and XII. See TPR 8 fig. 1, AVM DS 2 97). This type of pin is dated to the Early Dynastic III period at Tell Chuēra and Sargonid and Predynastic Graves at Ur. Parallels have also been uncovered at Til-Barsib and Selenkahiye.

Jewelry consists of earrings, TPR 8 21 and 22, and a bronze ring, TPR 8 23. Parallels for the shape of the rings and earrings come from Pre-Sargonid and Sargonid period graves at Ur, the Akkadian level at Tell Chuēra, ca. 2500 B.C. at Mari, Early Dynastic and Akkadian levels at Tell Brak, Chagar Bazar, and Tepe Gawra. One oval bronze ring or bracelet was excavated from Area B. Tureau-Dangin and Dunand (1936) suggests that such rings may have been cut and used as money (for the latest study of this problem see Powell, forthcoming).

A bronze axe, a leaf-shaped blade, and a tanged arrowhead represent the weapons excavated. The hafted axe, TPR 8 25, was the gift of a local resident, Mr. 'Asia Dhiab. The best analogy from Mari came from room 104 and is dated to the beginning of the second millennium (Parrot, 1959, Pg. 85). The leaf-shaped blade, TPR 8 26, with low central midrib, has parallels during the third millennium at Tell Chuēra, Chagar Bazar, the beginning of the second millennium at Mari, Ur, Til-Barsib, and the Old Babylonian levels at

---

* This saw, as seen in the 1979 excavations, came from a subsidiary room (STCD2) of the Temple of Ninkarrak. It may have had a utilitarian purpose, but could also have been a cult item associated with Ninkarrak or Shamash. – Editor's note.

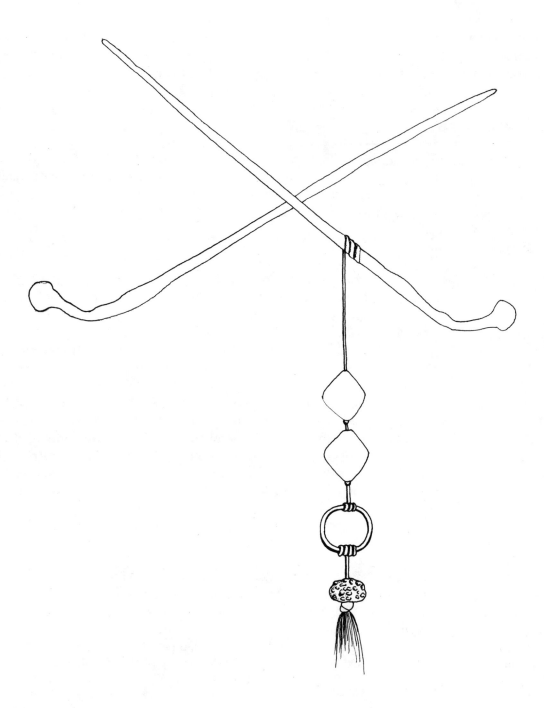

Figure 2.   Reconstruction of pins, beads, metal ring, and inlaid bead found in the third millennium shaft grave (1:2).

Nuzi. The saw, TPR 8 28, comes from SG 10, the Khana level, and is complete. Hafted into an antler or bone handle, it has a serrated edge and a rounded tip. The best parallel is the gold saw from Queen Shub-ad's Grave at Ur, although this example is much earlier than ours. (Woolley, 1934, Pl. 158). Other metal tools include a pair of tweezers, TRP 8 29, one possible axe, ingot, or weight, TPR 8 30, and several tubular bronze shafts of unknown use.

2.4 Miscellaneous Ceramic Implements

A number of miscellaneous ceramic objects including jar stoppers, wheels, a cart box or chariot, amulets, a container, possible catapults or sling balls, and a token were found during the excavation.

Two jar stoppers, TPR 8 35 and 36, were made of white gypsum with rounded tops and cylindrical plugs, and are similar to the "mushroom stoppers" excavated by Parrot at Mari (Parrot, 1959, fig. 98). The third example, TPR 8 37, is ceramic with a square, flat top and flaring sides. Similar jar stoppers have been excavated at both Mari and Nuzi. Seven clay wheels were excavated, all of which had raised hubs, rounded central perforations, and sloping sides; they are identical to the ones excavated during the second season. A ceramic cart box or chariot, TPR 8 39, rectangular in shape with a flat bottom and flaring sides, incised with linear incisions on the exterior was found in Area B. Many similar cart boxes have been excavated at Mari, Khan Sheikhoun, Tell Chuëra, Kish, Selenkahiye, Hama, and Harran. Other objects include ceramic disc, TPR 8 42, of light brown clay with a rounded central perforation from SG 11 and one soft, chalk disc, TPR 8 41, flat on one side and curved on the other, with a central perforation from SG 6. Two sling balls or catapults of ceramic were found in SG 14 and SG 20. One, TPR 8 43, is crudely egg-shaped. The other, TPR 8 44, is oval with two slightly flattened sides. Starr refers to these as clay counters (Starr 1937, Pl. 39). One possible token, TPR 8 51, is a half sphere, and similar to examples discussed by D. Schmandt-Besserat 1977, pg. 26.

2.5 Shell, Stone, and Bone Objects

Many drilled shells were excavated. All have been identified as local fresh water mollusks or as shells of Mediterranean origin. Species include *Dentalium novemcostatus* Lamarck, *Arcularia gibbonsula* Linnaeus, *Conus (Lautoconus) mediterraneus* Bruguiere, *Spondylus gaedaropus* Linnaeus, *Unio requienii* (?) Linnaeus, and *Acanthocardia rustica* Linnaeus. An incised mother-of-pearl shell pendant, TPR 8 56, was excavated from burial 1 in SG 14 next to the forehead. The curved top is incised with three sets of concentric circles while the back is undecorated. Similar round, white pendants are depicted on later paintings at Mari (Parrot, 1958, Pl. XXIII and Fig. 19 fragment B and 1959, Fig. 54 and Pl. XXVIII).

A number of stone beads of various shapes and colors were found in all areas of excavation. Two were rhomboids, TPR 8 57 and 58, excavated in connection with the burial 1 complex in SG 14. They were associated with the globular headed pins, bronze ring, and gypsum inlaid bead mentioned in the above text. Similar beads have been excavated at Tell Brak and date to the Sargonid period, the "A" Cemetery at Kish, the Early Dynastic III period at Tell Chuëra, and Ur in the Royal Cemetery. Many fine shell or gypsum beads excavated around the hips and skull area of the same burial complex suggests that a girdle or belt and hair piece of beads may have been worn. Similar strands of beads were excavated from Shub-ad's grave around the Queen's neck and shoulders. One blue paste bead from SG 9, TPR 8 83, with a ribbed top and flat base, and longitudinally pierced is similar to a ribbed frit bead from Nuzi. One blue glazed composition "fly pendant" was excavated in a mixed Islamic-Old Babylonian pit. A similar example was identified at Nuzi (Starr 1937, Pl. 120:VV). One haematite scale weight, similar to the one excavated during the second season, was found in SG 10.

One gypsum container, TPR 8 87, full of bitumen (?) beads was uncovered adjacent to the skull in SG 14 burial 1. It is not possible to reconstruct the original shape because it is so badly deteriorated. Seven beads were impressed into the porous mass and the imprints of several other beads were visible.

Bone tools and objects include six awls, one hollow tube, one ring, and one unusual amulet or gaming piece. The amulet, TPR 8 96, is scoop-shaped and has a long perforated rectangular shaft. It is decorated with several sets of concentrically incised circles.

3. Descriptive Catalog

3.1 Introduction

The Catalog consists of two basic parts, placed side by side: a verbal description and a graphic representation of the objects (for fuller description of this catalog see TPR 4). The verbal description is divided into three columns which include the following:

Designation and Documentation. Each object in the catalog is given a TPR 8 number followed by the type of object it is and then by the field (register) number which has the prefix TQ3-. Following this is the Deir ez-Zor Museum number (DeZ), the figure number in the catalog, and the illustration whenever applicable. The abbreviation AVM DS 2 refers to the slide number of that object.

Dimensions and Stratigraphy. The height (H) or length (L), width (W), thickness (Th), or diameter (D) are cited for each object in centimeters. Only essential stratigraphic designations are listed. For a fuller discussion of the stratigraphy, see TPR 6.

Description and Date. A brief description is given for each object, including material, decoration, and technical aspects of the object's manufacture. A date based on the stratigraphic position of the object and comparative material is cited. Photographic illustrations of the objects are presented separately in the plates.

Comparative Material. Whenever relevant, we have provided documentation on similar objects excavated elsewhere.

Figures. All drawings are 1:1 unless otherwise indicated.

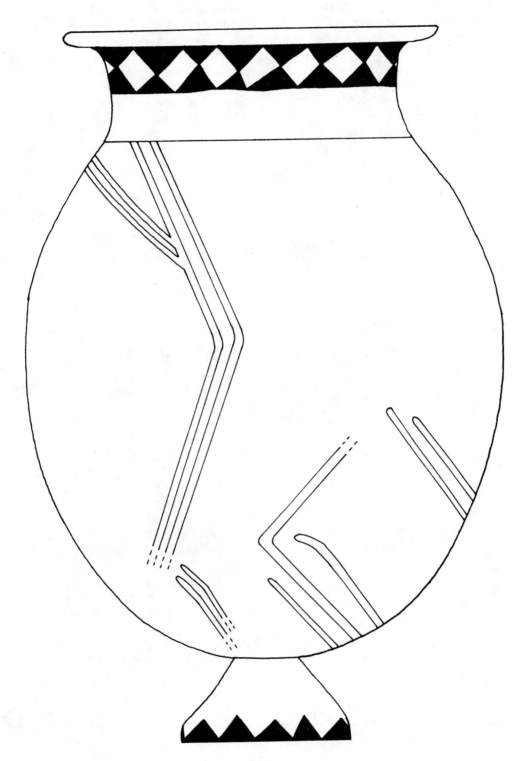

TPR 8 1

Figure 3

Designation and Documentation	Dimensions and Stratigraphy	Description and Date
TPR 8 1 Ostrich Egg TQ3-296 DeZ-1709 Fig. 3 Ill. 3	H: 15.3 T: 0.18 D: 13.0 Fragmented SG14, Locus 1, Burial 1, Level 7	One hundred and forty nine fragments, cream to caramel color. White striations from weathering or binding? Ceramic rim and base located with the egg. Mid-third millennium.

Comparative Material

Kish: Mackay 1925, Vol. I, Pg. 19
                              II, Pg. 136

Mari: Parrot 1956, Pl. LXXI:a

Nuzi: Starr 1937-39, Vol. I, Pg. 488

Terqa: Thureau-Dangin and Dhorme, 1924, Pl. LX Fig. 1

Ur: Woolley 1934, Vol. II, Text. Pgs. 56, 59, 60, 90, 96,
              113, 132, 152, 166-67, 173; Vol. II Plates, Pl. 156,
              U. 9255; Pl. 170:a.

Designation and Documentation	Dimensions and Stratigraphy	Description and Date
TPR 8 2 Rim of Ostrich Egg TQ3-294 DeZ-1707 Fig. 4a and b	H: 1.8 T: 9.27 D: 10.0 Lip W: 1.5 SG14, Locus 1, Burial 1, Level 7, Used as base for TQ3-296	Ceramic ring-shaped rim for ostrich egg. Cylindrical neck tapers slightly to egg. Broken. Light reddish-brown clay. Smooth surface originally inlaid with triangular pieces of mother-of-pearl shell. Inlay on top of rim and under lip. Traces of bitumen used to adhere inlay. Ca. 125 pieces. Mid-third millennium.
TPR 8 3 Ostrich Egg Stand TQ3-170 DeZ-1583 Fig. 4 Ill. 5	H: 2.1 Th: ca. 0.3 D: base 4.9 rim 1.9 SG14, Locus 1, Burial 1, Level 7	Cone-shaped stand. Open at both ends. Finger smoothed. Reddish-brown clay slipped with dark brown. Slip flaking off. Inlaid with triangular pieces of mother-of-pearl. Mid-third millennium.

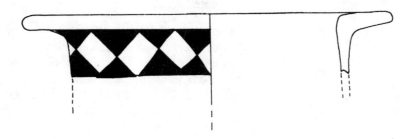

TPR 8 2a (profile)

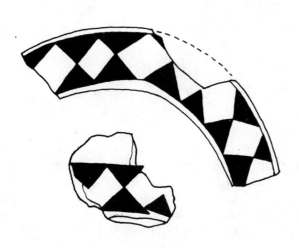

TPR 8 2b (top view)

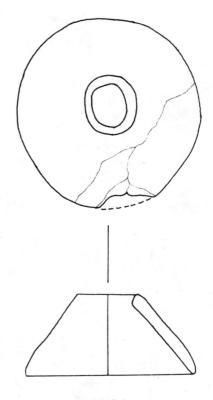

TPR 8 3

Figure 4

Designation and Documentation	Dimensions and Stratigraphy	Description and Date
TPR 8 4 Female Figurine head? TQ3-380 DeZ-1793 Fig. 5 Ill. 6 AVM DS 2 34	H: 2.8 W: 3.2 Th: 2.26 SF 34	Handmade clay head. Female with beaked nose. Broken below neck. Two round pellet eyes with round central perforations. Traces of black paint around eyes. Eighteen parallel incisions across forehead indicating hair. Applied pellet necklace around front of neck, filled with short diagonal incisions. Back is undecorated. Light brown clay with sand temper. Possibly an owl? Date unknown.

Comparative Material

Chagar Bazar:	Mallowan 1937, Fig. 9:4
Tell Chuēra:	Moortgat 1960, Pg. 43, Abb. 43 a, b, c
Harran:	Prag 1970, Fig. 9:70
Mari:	Parrot 1956, Pl. LXVIII: 133, 649 and 399
Tello:	Barrelet 1968, Pl. LII: 548
Selenkahiye:	Van Loon 1973, Pg. 155, Fig. 7
Ur:	Woolley and Mallowan 1976, Pl. 65

Designation and Documentation	Dimensions and Stratigraphy	Description and Date
TPR 8 5 Female Figurine TQ3-23 DeZ-1436 Fig. 5 Ill. 7	H: 7.5 W: 4.0 Th: 2.3 SG 8, FT 5, Level 3	Fragment of crude handmade nude figurine, broken at waist. Bitumen traces on broken ends. Navel indicated by shallow depression. Incised line below navel. Pubic triangle with hair indicated by short, diagonal stabs. Two incised lines and two dimples on back. Pronounced buttocks. Rounded legs fused together. Date unknown.

Comparative Material.

Mari:	Parrot 1959, Pg. 63: fig. 52; Pl. LXVIII: Nos. 372, 433 and 50 Parrot 1956, Pl. LXVIII:38, 50, 372

Designation and Documentation	Dimensions and Stratigraphy	Description and Date
TPR 8 6 Plaque? TQ3-237 DeZ-1649 Fig. 5	H: 6.7 W: 4.0 Th: 1.9 SG 7, Locus 25, Level 9	Crude, hand modeled. Applied pellet pendant (?) with wing-shaped pellets to either side. Many punctations on pellet surfaces. Curved top has two depressions. Stands freely on flat base to which something was adhered. Light green to buff colored clay. Khana period.

TPR 8 4

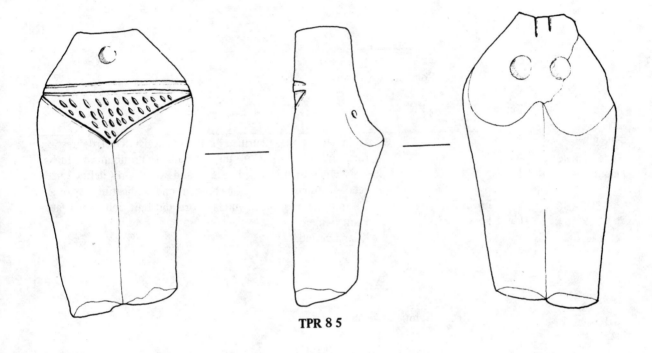

TPR 8 5

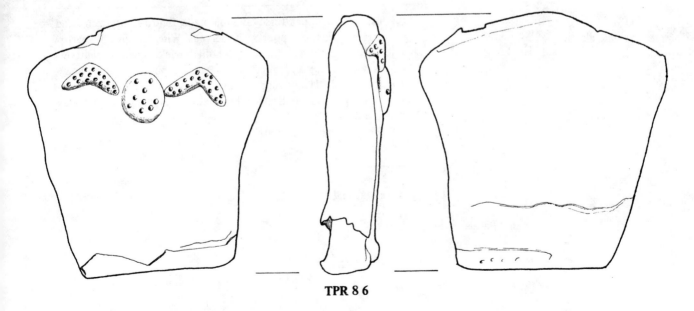

TPR 8 6

Figure 5

SMS 3, 47

Designation and Documentation	Dimensions and Stratigraphy	Description and Date
TPR 8 7 Nude Female Plaque TQ3-365 DeZ-1778 Fig. 6	H: 3.05 W: 3.7 Th: 2.14 SG 19, Locus 2 Level 3, FT 7	Moldmade. Hips and thighs preserved. Well modelled. Back of plaque finger smoothed. Date unknown.
	Comparative Material	
	Terqa: TPR 3 2	
TPR 8 8 Nude Female Plaque TQ3-236 DeZ-1648 Fig. 6 Ill. 8	H: 10.2 W: 3.2 Th: 1.5 SG 7, Locus 24, Level 11	Moldmade nude figurine, broken at waist. Oval depression for navel. "V" shaped pubic triangle. Pronounced thighs. Legs taper to undefined feet. Stands on poorly defined pedestal. Bitumen traces on broken end indicating repair in antiquity. Reddish brown clay core and buff colored surface. Plant temper. Khana period.
	Comparative Material	
	Tello: Barrelet 1968; Pl. XLI:428	
TPR 8 9 Female Plaque TQ3-364 DeZ-1777 Fig. 6 Ill. 9	H: 4.3 W: 3.3 Th: 1.9 CF	Head and upper torso of moldmade figurine. Stylized head. Facial features poorly preserved. Wide forehead, narrow cheeks, pointed chin. Hair pulled back. Figure's right eye has round incised pupil. Left eye is a bump. Faintly incised eyebrows. Hands cup breasts. Figure's arms have incised lines possibly indicating bracelets. Light red to buff clay. Sand temper. Possibly Khana period.
	Comparative Material	
	Chagar Bazar: Mallowan 1947, Pl. LV:5	
	Tello: Barrelet 1968, Pl. XXXVII:387	
	Uruk: Ziegler 1962, Pl. II:173	

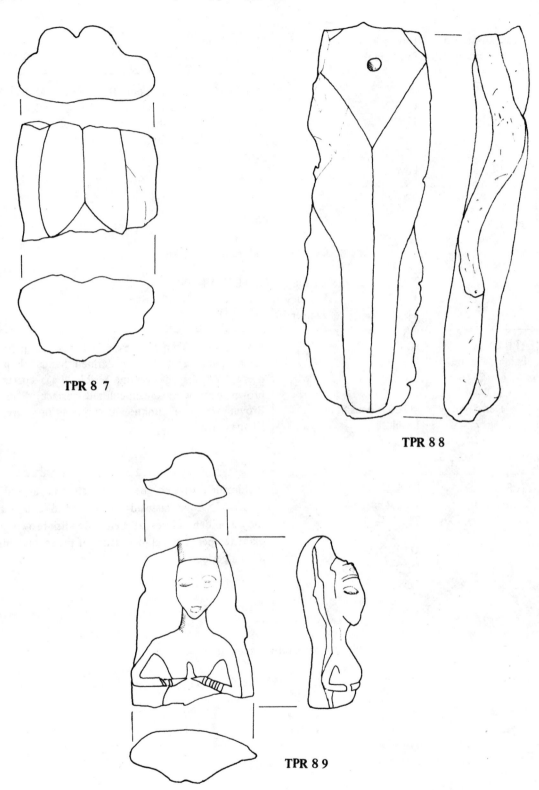

TPR 8 7

TPR 8 8

TPR 8 9

Figure 6

SMS 3, 49

Designation and Documentation	Dimensions and Stratigraphy	Description and Date
TPR 8 10 Female Plaque TQ3-165 DeZ-1578 Fig. 6 Ill. 10	H: 4.7 W: 3.25 Th: 2.0 SG 9, Locus 3, Level 3	Moldmade head fragment. Broken edge at neck has traces of bitumen. Bangs across forehead. Locks on each side of face. Nose broken. Lozenge-shaped grooves for eyes. No ears. Indistinct lips. Poorly preserved. Khana period.

Comparative Material

Tello:	Barrelet 1968, Pl. XLVI:490
Ur:	Woolley and Mallowan 1976, Pl. 68: 38
Uruk:	Ziegler 1962, Pl. II:171

Designation and Documentation	Dimensions and Stratigraphy	Description and Date
TPR 8 11 Female Plaque TQ3-244 DeZ-1656 Fig. 7 Ill. 11 AVM DS 2 32	H: 8.4 W: 3.1 Th: 1.8 SG 20, Locus 5, Level 2	Moldmade. Broken at neck and knees. Garment raised to reveal pubic area. Poorly defined hands clasp sides of dress. "V" shaped neckline visible. Legs apart. Reddish-brown clay with cream-colored surface. Plant temper. Brown flakes of unknown composition cover surface. Khana period.
TPR 8 12 Plaque with Male Figure TQ3-414 DeZ-1827 Fig. 7 Ill. 12	H: 4.24 W: 4.4 Th: 1.7 SG 19, STC A1 FT 32, Locus 9, Level 12	Moldmade. Broken below waist and at ankles. Well preserved. Long tasseled robe, fringed end draped over the shoulder. Flares at hem. Reddish-brown clay with plant temper. Typical male attire of the second millennium. Khana period.

Comparative Material

Mari:	Parrot 1959, Fig. 13; description of a robe Pgs. 19-20 Pl. I; Pl. IX
Ur:	Woolley and Mallowan 1976, Pl. 3:88
Louvre:	Strommenger 1964, Pl. 143

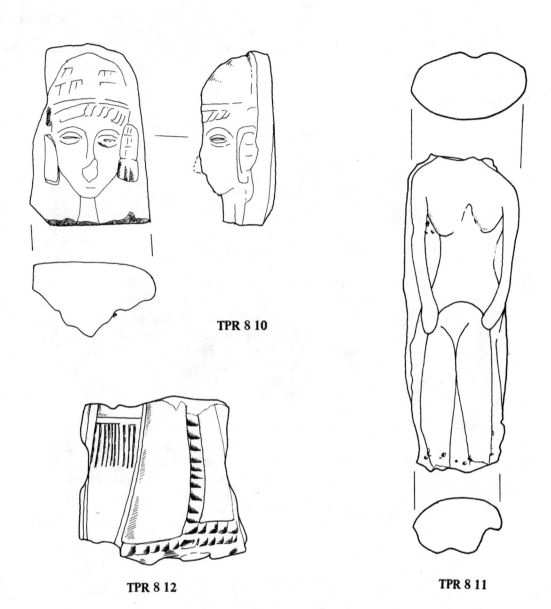

TPR 8 10

TPR 8 12

TPR 8 11

Figure 7

Designation and Documentation	Dimensions and Stratigraphy	Description and Date
TPR 8 13 Quadruped TQ3-93 DeZ-1506 Fig. 8 Ill. 13 AVM DS 2 33	L: 8.1 H: 4.9 W: 3.0 SG 15, Level 2	Clay, crude hand modeling. Horns and tail. Hole perforated through head for reins or perhaps indicating eyes. Head turned slightly to the left. Rounded, tapered legs. Tips of two legs pinched to indicate hooves. Elongated torso with broad fore and hindquarters. Light brown clay. Possibly mid-third millennium.
		————
	Comparative Material	
	Tell Al'Abd Zrejehey: Tell Chuẽra: Tepe Gawra: Selenkahiye:	Toueir 1978, Pls. IX:77; XII:251 Moortgat 1962, Abb. 12a Speiser 1935, Pl. XXXIV:C, No. 7 Van Loon, 1968, Pgs. 28-29
TPR 8 14 Animal Head TQ3-285 DeZ-1698 Fig. 8	H: 5.6 D: 3.4 SG 18, FT 4, Locus 1, Level 6	Crude, schematic animal head with elongated neck. Triangular head. Two ears and snout eroded. Rounded central perforation. Possibly a vessel spout? Cream colored clay with sand and vegetable temper. Khana period.
TPR 8 15 Clay Hoof TQ3-234 DeZ-1646 Fig. 8	H: 3.6 W: 2.6 SF near SG 10	Crude handmade cloven hoof. Hoof delineated by two slanting incised lines forming a "V" and one deep central groove below. Oval cross-section. Stumpy. Reddish brown clay with cream colored slip. Plant temper. Date unknown.
		————
	Comparative Material	
	Uruk:	Heinrich 1936, Pl. 14d

TPR 8 13

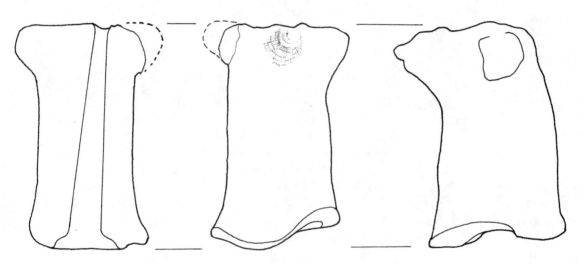

TPR 8 14

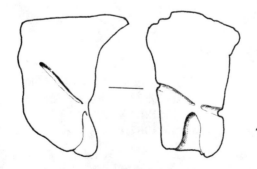

TPR 8 15

Figure 8

Designation and Documentation	Dimensions and Stratigraphy	Description and Date

TPR 8 16
Pin Fragment
 	
  TQ3-117
  DeZ-1530
  Fig. 9
	L: 2.55
	Th: 0.6
	
	SG 9, Locus 4,
	Level 3
		Corroded fragment of shaft. Bronze?
		Khana period.

TPR 8 17
Pin
  TQ3-259
  DeZ-1672
  Fig. 9
  Ill. 14
	L: 16.0
	D: 0.34
	SG 7, Locus 26
	Level 10
		Corroded and covered with green oxidation, which has flaked off in some areas, exposing core. Shaft is bent. Round cross-section. Bronze?
		Khana period.

TPR 8 18
Pin
 	
  TQ3-227
  DeZ-1639
  Fig. 9
  Ill. 15
	L: 8.9
	W: 0.5
	
	SG 10, FT 14,
	firepit, Level 6
		Spiral headed pin, rectangular in cross-section. Tapers to a point. Bronze?
		Khana period.

———

Comparative Material

Alalakh:	Woolley 1955, pin type 11:Pl. LXXIII	
Til-Barsib:	Thureau-Dangin and Dunand 1936, Pl. XXX:3	
Tell Brak:	Mallowan 1947, Pl. XXXI:6	
Chagar Bazar:	Mallowan 1937, Fig. 12:8	
Mari:	Parrot 1959, Pg. 94: Fig. 69:790	
Ur:	Woolley 1934, Pls. 218 and 231	

Designation and Documentation	Dimensions and Stratigraphy	Description and Date

TPR 8 19
Globular Headed Pin
 	
  TQ3-152, 155
  DeZ-1565, 1568
  Fig. 9
  Ill. 16
  AVM DS 2 97
	L: 29.1
	D: 0.45
	D of head: 1.5
	
	SG 14, Locus 1,
	  Burial 1,
	  Level 7
		Corroded globular headed pin. Hole pierced through shaft. Bent above perforation. Round cross-section. Tapers to a point.
		Mid-third millennium

———

Comparative Material

Til-Barsib:	Thureau-Dangin and Dunand 1936, Pl. XXX:4	
Tell Chuēra:	Moortgat 1965, Pg. 42 and 44, Abb. 30 and 31	
Mari:	Parrot 1959, Pg. 94, Fig. 69:721	
	1961, Pl. XI:2, 3, 4	
Selenkahiye:	Van Loon 1967, Pg. 30	
Ur:	Woolley 1934, Pl. 231:b/c, type 7 pins; Pl. 60	

Designation and Documentation	Dimensions and Stratigraphy	Description and Date

TPR 8 20
Globular Headed Pin
 	
  TQ 3-153, 154
  DeZ-1566, 1567
  Fig. 9
  Ill. 17
	L: 29.1
	D: 0.75
	D of head: 1.5
	
	SG 14, Locus 1,
	  Burial 1,
	  Level 7
		Corroded globular headed pin. Round hole pierces shank near head of pin. Curved above perforation. Round cross-section. Tapers to a point. See TPR 8 19.
		Mid-third millennium.

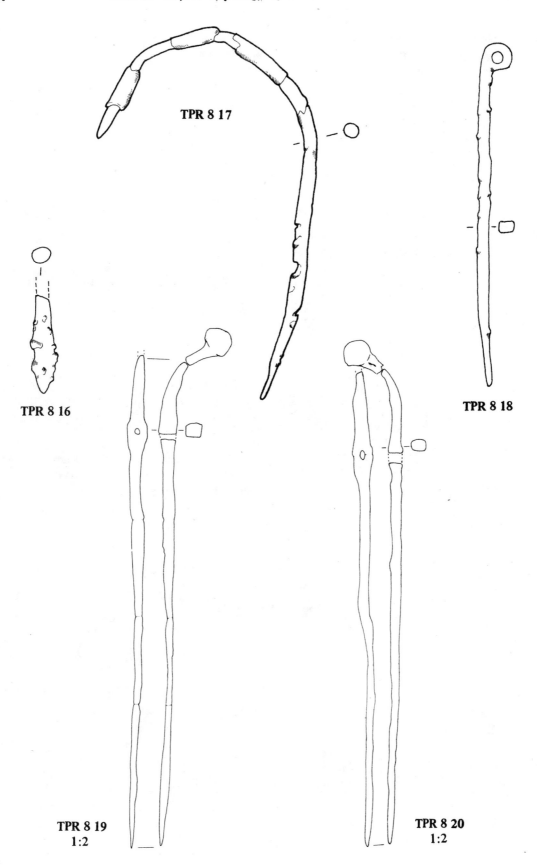

TPR 8 17

TPR 8 16

TPR 8 18

TPR 8 19
1:2

TPR 8 20
1:2

Figure 9

SMS 3, 55

Designation and Documentation	Dimensions and Stratigraphy	Description and Date
TPR 8 21 Earring? TQ3-390 DeZ-1803 Fig. 10 Ill. 18	D: 0.77 Th: 0.2 SG 19, STC A1, FT 20, Locus 5,	Small, oval earring with ends crossed. Round cross-section. Bronze? Khana period.

Comparative Material

Tell Brak:	Mallowan 1947, Pl. XXXIII:5 and 6;	
Chagar Bazar:	Mallowan 1937, Pl. XIII: Fig. a 1947, Pl. LIII:38	
Mari:	Parrot 1956, Pl. LXIV:608 and 109; Pl. LXII:640	
Tepe Gawra:	Speiser 1935, Pl. LXXXII:24	
Ur:	Woolley 1934, Vol. II Plates Pl. 146:c; Pl. 219; Vol. II Text, Pgs. 128 and 243	

TPR 8 22 Earring? TQ3-284 DeZ-1697 Fig. 10	D; 1.7 Th: 0.4 SG 20, Locus 8, Level 4	Corroded. Ends broken, but probably overlapped as TPR 8 21. Bronze? Khana period.
TPR 8 23 Ring TQ3-175 DeZ-1587 Fig. 10 Ill. 19	D: 2.5 Th: 0.2 SG 14, Locus 1, Burial 1, Level 7	Round. Ends fastened together. Corroded surface. Thin piece of metal over fastened ends. Bronze? Mid-third millennium.

Comparative Material

Ur:	Woolley 1934, Pl. 226	

TPR 8 24 Bracelet or Section of Currency coil? TQ3-290 DeZ-1703 Fig. 10 Ill. 20	Th: 0.3 D: 6.25 SG 20, Locus 8, Level 4.	Corroded. Rounded cross-section. Incomplete. One end hammered flat. Oval shape. Possibly sliced for use as currency. (Powell in press). Bronze? Possibly Khana period.

Comparative Material

Til-Barsib:	Thureau-Dangin and Dunand 1936, Album Pl. XVIII:2 and 3; Text Pg. 108:33	
Tepe Gawra:	Speiser 1935, Pl. LXXXII:22	

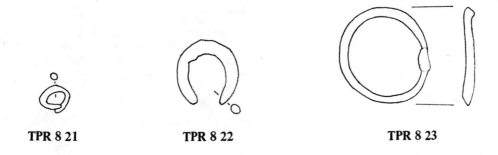

TPR 8 21   TPR 8 22   TPR 8 23

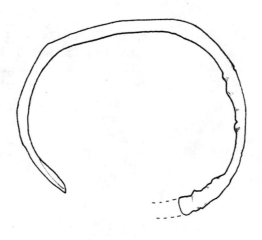

TPR 8 24

Figure 10

Designation and Documentation	Dimensions and Stratigraphy	Description and Date
TPR 8 25 Axe TQ3-34 DeZ-1447 Fig. 11 Ill. 21 AVM DS 2 102	L: 15.5 W: 4.0 H: 4.5 CF 1	Wedge-shaped blade. One cutting edge. Damaged from use. Hafted at one end. Haft has three horizontal ridges. Haft pierced by ragged holes. Bronze? Mid-third millennium.
		Comparative Material
	Mari:	Parrot 1956, Pg. 139 Fig. 80:474 1959, Fig. 65:993; Fig. 54:1507, Pg. 85
TPR 8 26 Spear TQ3-360 DeZ-1773 Fig. 11 Ill. 22 AVM DS 2 37	L: 11.9 W: 2.2 Th: 0.4 SG 19, STC A1 FT 31, Locus 4, Level 11	Leaf-shaped blade. Central mid-rib. Haft narrow and rectangular in cross-section. Bronze? Khana period.
		Comparative Material
	Til-Barsib:	Thureau-Dangin 1936, Album Pl. XXX:12; Text Pg. 107:20
	Chagar Bazar:	Mallowan 1937, Pl. XIV, Fig. E
	Tell Chuēra:	Moortgat 1962, Abb. 29, Pg. 37
	Nuzi:	Starr 1939, Pl. 125
TPR 8 27 Tanged Arrowhead TQ3-355 DeZ-1768 Fig. 11 Ill. 23 AVM DS 2 36	L: 2.73 W: 2.05 Haft stem: 0.96 SG 19, STC A1, FT 31, Locus 4, Level 11	Asymmetrical. One edge long and thin, other edge blunt and rounded. Tip pointed. Haft flares slightly. Khana period.

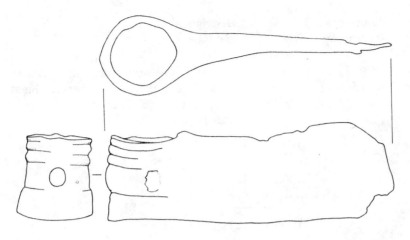

TPR 8 25
1:2

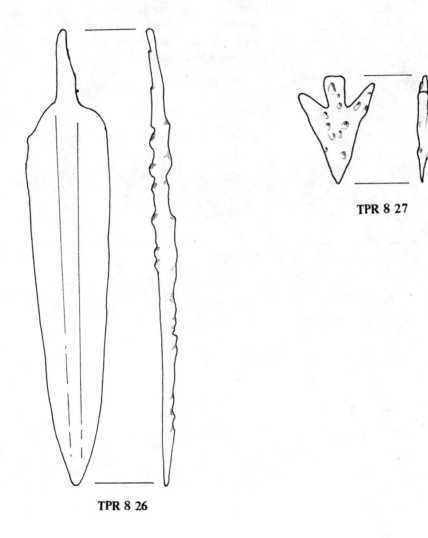

TPR 8 27

TPR 8 26

Figure 11

Designation and Documentation	Dimensions and Stratigraphy	Description and Date
TPR 8 28 Saw TQ3-100 DeZ-1513 Fig. 12 Ill. 24 AVM DS 2 39	L: 36.7 W: 5.5 Th: 0.2 (blade) SG 10, FT 9, Level 4	Complete saw with antler or bone handle. One serrated cutting edge. Hafted into handle. Blunt, rounded point. Handle cracked. Blade bronze? Khana period.

Comparative Material

Ur: Woolley 1934, Vol. II Plates Pl. 158:b Vol. II Text
              see Pg. 303. (Gold, Early Dynastic period)

Designation and Documentation	Dimensions and Stratigraphy	Description and Date
TPR 8 29 Tweezers? TQ3-77 DeZ-1490 Fig. 12 Ill. 25	L: 4.0 W: 0.8 H: 0.7 SG 8, Locus 18, Level 5	Corroded copper or bronze object, possibly tweezers. Two parallel blades, close together. Square in cross-section. Blades slightly apart on one end. Possibly Khana period.
TPR 8 30 Axe? TQ3-209 DeZ-1621 Fig. 12 Ill. 26 AVM DS 2 38	L: 6.8 W: 3.0 Th: 1.5 SG 9, FT 6, Level 2	Bronze? Axe, weight, or ingot. Corroded surface. Weathered edges.

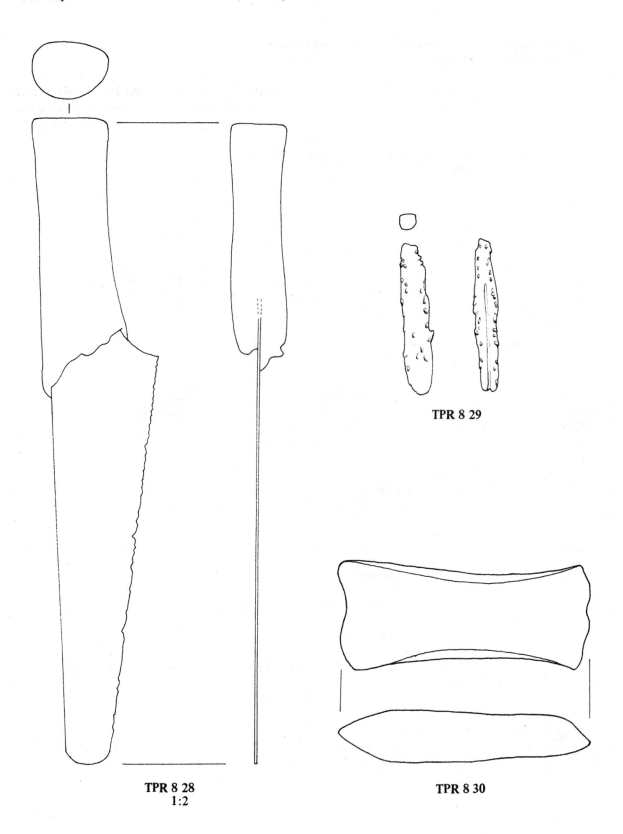

TPR 8 29

TPR 8 28
1:2

TPR 8 30

Figure 12

Designation and Documentation	Dimensions and Stratigraphy	Description and Date
TPR 8 31 Shaft TQ3-361 DeZ-1774 Fig. 13	L: 11.3 D: 1.0 SG 19, STC A1 FT 31, Locus 4 Level 11	Tubular shaft, broken. Very corroded. Possibly used as wine strainer. Band around perimeter. One end tapers to point. Tip broken. Three tiny holes run along axis. Bronze? Khana period.
	Comparative Material Chagar Bazar: Mallowan 1937, Pl. XIV:c	
TPR 8 32 Shaft TQ3-417 DeZ-1830 Fig. 13	L: 6.7 D: 1.0 Th: 0.12 SG 7, STC B1, FT 25, Locus 32, Level 12	Hollow shaft. Ends broken. Corroded. Bronze? Khana period.
TPR 8 33 Shaft TQ3-441 DeZ-1854 Fig. 13	L: 6.8 D: 1.0 Th: 0.4 SG 7, STC B1 Locus 34, Level 12	Tubular shaft, broken. Corroded. One end tapers to blunt point. Bronze? Khana period.
	Comparative Material Mari: Parrot 1956, Pl. LXIV: 353 Nuzi: Starr 1937, Pl. 125:K	
TPR 8 34 Tool? TQ3-376 DeZ-1789 Fig. 13	L: 5.68 D: 0.27 SG 19, STC B1 FT 33, Locus 8, Level 9	Corroded shaft with pointed tip. Square cross section. End broken. Bronze? Khana period.

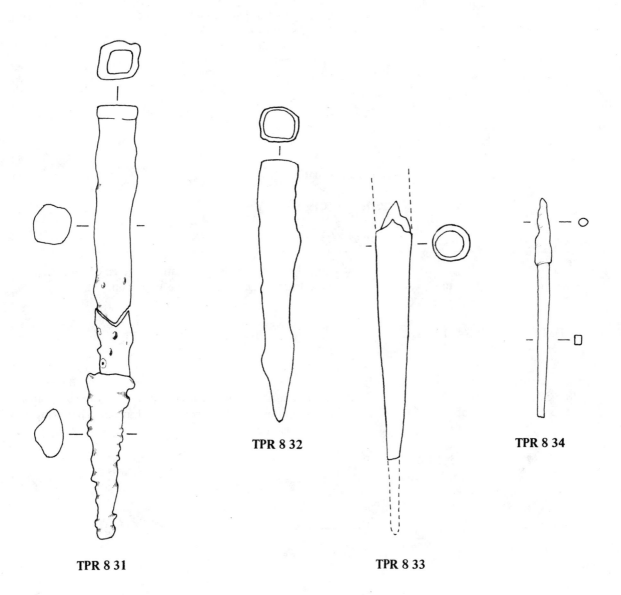

TPR 8 31

TPR 8 32

TPR 8 33

TPR 8 34

Figure 13

Designation and Documentation	Dimensions and Stratigraphy	Description and Date
TPR 8 35 Jar Stopper TQ3-391 DeZ-1804 Fig. 14	H: 5.9 D: 11.9 D of plug: 8.4 SG 19, FT 12, Locus 5	Soft white plaster. Crudely rounded. Top has small round knob. Stopper broken. Cylindrical plug. Possibly Khana period. Comparative Material Mari: Parrot 1959, Pg. 144, fig. 98 Nuzi: Starr 1937, Pl. 95:D
TPR 8 36 Jar Stopper TQ3-66 DeZ-1479 Fig. 14 Ill. 27	H: 8.25 D of top: 11.0 D of plug: 8.0 SG 7, Locus 6, Level 2	Crudely made of white plaster. Top is curved. Plug is cylindrical. Finger prints visible around lip. Date unknown.
TPR 8 37 Jar Stopper TQ3-307 DeZ-1720 Fig. 14 Ill. 28	H: 4.3 D of top: 5.2 D of plug: 2.2 SG 18, FT 4, Locus 1, Level 6	Crudely made of brown clay. Square, flat top with flared edges and rounded corners. Top broken. Sand temper. Khana period. Mari: Parrot 1959, Fig. 95 Nuzi: Starr 1937, Pl. 95:F

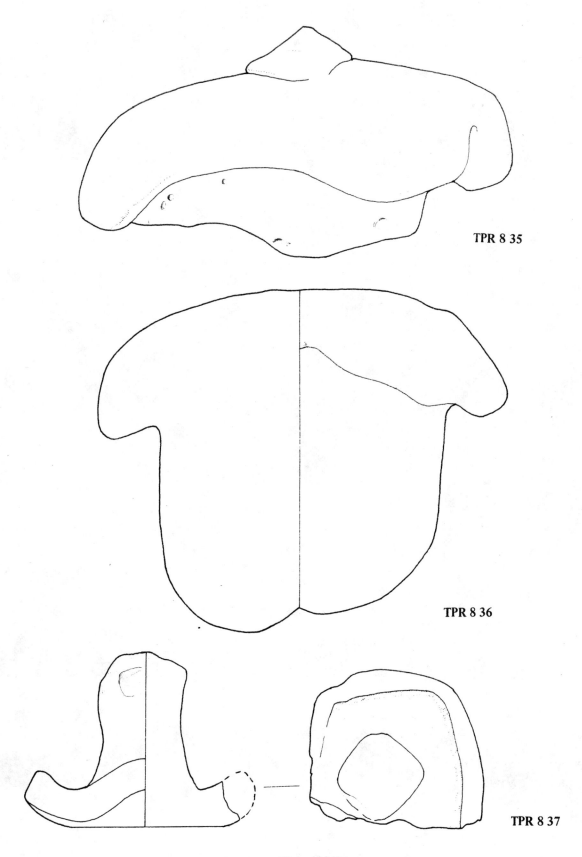

TPR 8 35

TPR 8 36

TPR 8 37

Figure 14

SMS 3, 65

1. Third millennium woman's shaft burial in SG 14. The complete
assemblage of grave offerings.

2. Close up of shaft burial in SG 14. Visible are two bronze pins, ostrich
egg, inlaid bead, two conoid beads, a bronze ring, and a
scattering of gypsum beads

3. TPR 8 1
(TQ3-296) Ostrich Egg

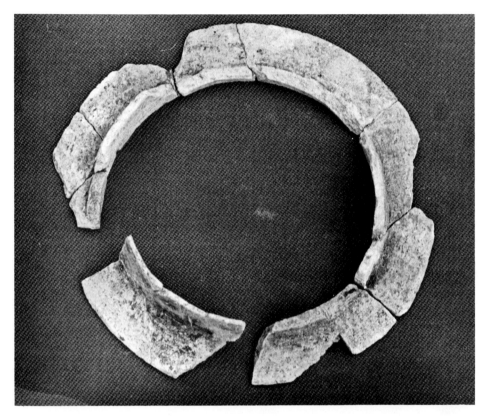

4a. TPR 8 2
(TQ3-294) Rim of Ostrich Egg

4b. TPR 8 2
(TQ3-294) Inlaid Rim

5. TPR 8 3
(TQ3-170) Stand

6. TPR 8 4
(TQ3-380) Female Figurine

7. TPR 8 5
(TQ3-23) Female Figurine

9. TPR 8 9
(TQ3-364) Female Figurine

10. TPR 8 10
(TQ3-165) Female Figurine

8. TPR 8 8
(TQ3-236) Female Figurine

11. TPR 8 11
(TQ3-244) Female Figurine

12. TPR 8 12
(TQ3-414) Male Figurine

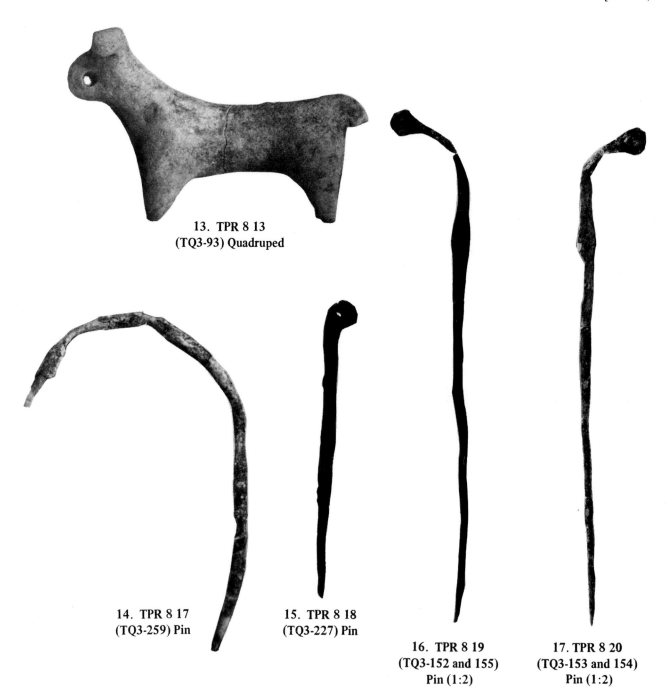

13. TPR 8 13
(TQ3-93) Quadruped

14. TPR 8 17
(TQ3-259) Pin

15. TPR 8 18
(TQ3-227) Pin

16. TPR 8 19
(TQ3-152 and 155)
Pin (1:2)

17. TPR 8 20
(TQ3-153 and 154)
Pin (1:2)

**18. TPR 8 21
(TQ3-390)
Earring**

**19. TPR 8 23
(TQ3-175) Ring**

**20. TPR 8-24
(TQ3-290) Bracelet**

**21. TPR 8-25
(TQ3-34)
Axe (1:2)**

23. TPR 8 27
(TQ3-355)
Arrowhead

25. TPR 8 29
(TQ3-77) Tweezers

22. TPR 8 26
(TQ3-360) Spear

26. TPR 8 30
(TQ3-209) Axe?

24. TPR 8 28
(TQ3-100) Saw
1:2

27. TPR 8 36
(TQ3-66) Stopper

28. TPR 8 37
(TQ3-307) Stopper

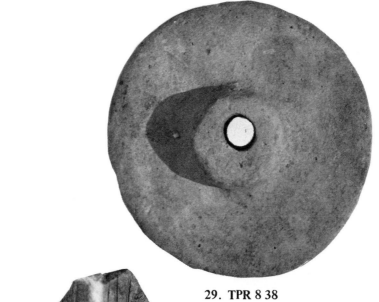

29. TPR 8 38
(TQ3-267) Toy Wheel

30. TPR 8 39
(TQ3-189) Cart Box

31. TPR 8 43
(TQ3-309) Sling Ball

32. TPR 8 47, 51, 53, 55
(TQ3-52, 291, 111, 116)
Drilled Shells

33. TPR 8 56
(TQ3-156) Shell Disc

34. TPR 8 57
(TQ3-176) Bead

35. TPR 8 58
(TQ3-168) Bead

36. TPR 8 73
(TQ3-129) Inlaid
Bead

37. TPR 8 74
(TQ3-171, 172 and 377)
Gypsum Beads

38. TPR 8 85
(TQ3-375)
Fly Pendant

39. TPR 8 86
(TQ3-166) Bead Container

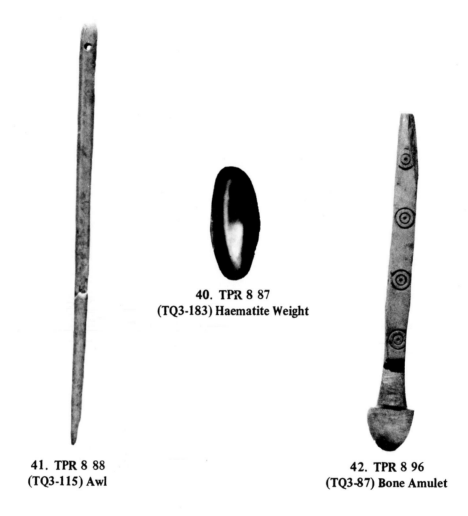

40. TPR 8 87
(TQ3-183) Haematite Weight

41. TPR 8 88
(TQ3-115) Awl

42. TPR 8 96
(TQ3-87) Bone Amulet

Designation and Documentation	Dimensions and Stratigraphy	Description and Date
TPR 8 38 Toy Wheel TQ3-267 DeZ-1680 Fig. 15 Ill. 29	D: 7.1 Th: 3.2 SG 17, FT 10, Level 3	Raised central hubs. Central hole. Medium brown clay. Khana period.
TPR 8 38a Toy Wheel TQ3-387 DeZ-1800	D: 5.55 Th: 3.1 SG 14, Locus 5, Level 7	Raised hubs. Rounded central hole. Light reddish brown clay core. Buff surface. Plant temper. Khana period.
TPR 8 38b Toy Wheel TQ3-379 DeZ-1792	D: 7.2 Th: 5.2 SG 17, Locus 6, Level 3	Raised hubs. Slanted central hole. Light brown clay with plant temper. Khana period.
TPR 8 38c Toy Wheel TQ3-220 DeZ-1632	D: 4.0 Th: 2.0 SG 11,	Raised central hubs. Rounded hole. Off-center. Bumpy, crude surface. Medium reddish brown clay. Khana period.
TPR 38d Toy Wheel TQ3-124 DeZ-1537	D: 10.98 Th: 4.3 SG 9, Burial 2, Level 3	Raised central hubs. Rounded central hole. Light brown clay surface with evidence of plant temper. Reddish firing cloud in one area. Khana period.
TPR 8 38e Toy Wheel TQ3-78 DeZ-1491	D: 4.3 Th: 1.45 SG 7, FT 8, Level 4	Raised central hubs. Rounded central perforation. Edges chipped. Possibly Khana period.
TPR 8 38f Toy Wheel TQ3-74 DeZ-1487	D: 11.0 Th: 4.4 SG 9, Locus 3, Level 3	Raised central hubs. Oval central perforation. Wheel diameter varies. Fragments of wheel edge and one hub missing. Smoothed surface. Plant temper. Khana period.

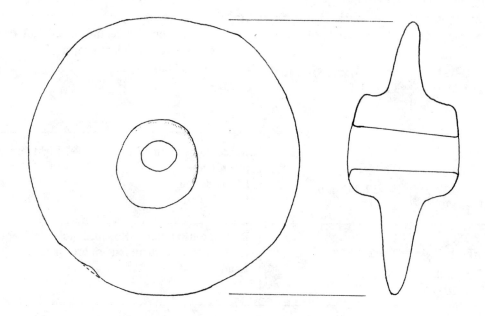

TPR 8 38

Figure 15

Designation and Documentation	Dimensions and Stratigraphy	Description and Date
TPR 8 39 Cart Box or Chariot TQ3-189 DeZ-1601 Fig. 16 Ill. 30	L: 5.5 H: 4.9 W: 4.9 SG 21, Surface Cleaning	Handmade rectangular-shaped container, probably a cart box or chariot. Flat bottom, flaring sides. Linear incisions on exterior. Rounded corners. Fragmented. Ceramic of light brown clay with sand temper. Date unknown.

Comparative Material

Tell Al'Abd   Toueir 1978, Pl. XX, Figs. 296 and 299;
Pl. XIX, Figs. 59, 106 and 295

Brak: Mallowan 1947, Pl. LXIV

Tell Chuēra: Moortgat 1960a, Abb. 44, Pg. 43
1962, Abb. 8, Pg. 13

Hama: Fugmann 1958, Pl. XII; 5; Fig. 139:b

Harran: Prag 1970, Pg. 89, Fig. 10: 80 and 81

Kish: Langdon 1924, Pl. VII, Fig. 3

Mari: Parrot 1959, Pg. 79, Fig. 62

Nuzi: Starr 1937, Pl. 54; Pl. 99

Khan Sheikhoun: Du Mesnil du Buisson 1932, Pl. XXXVI, Fig. 97

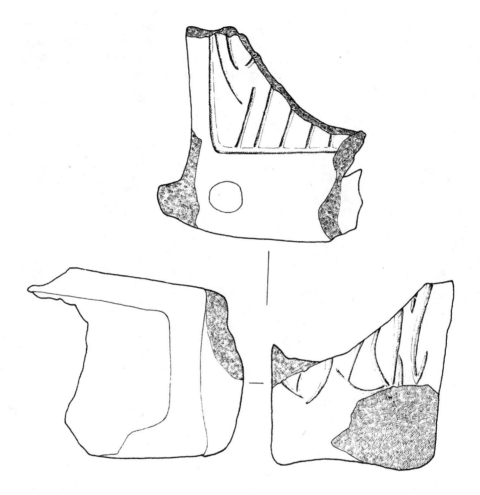

TPR 8 39

Figure 16

Designation and Documentation	Dimensions and Stratigraphy	Description and Date
TPR 8 40 Bead or Amulet TQ3-123 DeZ-1536 Fig. 17	D: 3.0 W: 2.6 Th: 1.2 SG 10, Locus 9, Level 4	Star-shaped. Seven points. Handmade. Round central hole. Ceramic. Possibly Khana period.
TPR 8 41 Chalk Disc TQ3-120 DeZ-1533 Fig. 17	D: 3.2 H: 0.95 SG 6, Locus 4, Level 5	White. Central perforation. One side flat. Other side rounded. Soft and porous. Khana period.
TPR 8 42 Ceramic Disc TQ3-205 DeZ-1617 Fig. 17	H: 1.05 D: 6.3 SG 11, Level 4	Handmade. Surface finger smoothed. Round perforation off-center. Light brown clay. Sand temper. Possibly a loom weight. Mid-third millennium.
TPR 8 43 Sling Ball or Catapult Ball? TQ3-309 DeZ-1722 Fig. 17 Ill. 31	L: 4.7 D: 3.2 SG 14, Locus 1, Level 7	Handmade, egg-shaped ceramic object, possibly a sling ball or catapult ball. Medium brown clay. Rough surface. Starr refers to these at Nuzi as clay counters. Mid-third millennium.

Comparative Material

Nuzi: Starr 1937, Pl. 39

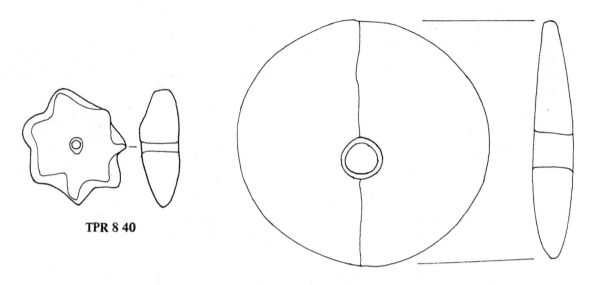

TPR 8 40

TPR 8 41

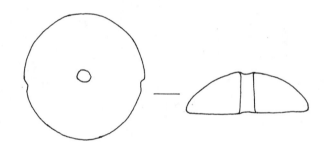

TPR 8 42

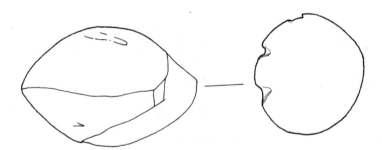

TPR 8 43

Figure 17

Designation and Documentation	Dimensions and Stratigraphy	Description and Date
TPR 8 44 Sling Ball or Catapult ball TQ3-394 DeZ-1807 Fig. 18	L: 4.6 W: 4.2 Th: 3.46 SG 20, Locus 2, Level 1	Rounded ceramic object. Two slightly flattened sides. Oval in cross-section. Medium reddish-brown clay with plant temper. Rough surface. Date unknown.
TPR 8 45 Possible Token TQ3-419 DeZ-1832 Fig. 18	D: 1.6 SG 19, STC A1, FT 22, Locus 5, Level 9	Spherical, fired clay token or bulla. Hand rolled. Ovoid. Smoothed surface. Buff colored clay. Sand temper. Khana period. ― Comparative Material D. Schmandt-Besserat 1977, chart 7 page 26
TPR 8 46 Shell Bead TQ3-109 DeZ-1522 Fig. 18	L: 4.03 W: 0.15 SG 6, Locus 2, Level 5	*Dentalium novemcostatus* Lamarck. Polished exterior. Khana period.
TPR 8 47 Drilled Shell TQ3-52 DeZ-1465 Fig. 18 Ill. 32	L: 1.4 W: 0.8 SG 6, Locus 3, Level 2	*Arcularia gibbosula* Linnaeus. Mediterranean origin. Central perforation. Polished. Khana period.
TPR 8 48 Drilled Shell TQ3-142 DeZ-1555 Fig. 18	L: 1.8 W: 1.5 H: 1.4 SG 6, Locus 4, Level 7	Snail with perforation near opening. Cream colored. Khana period.

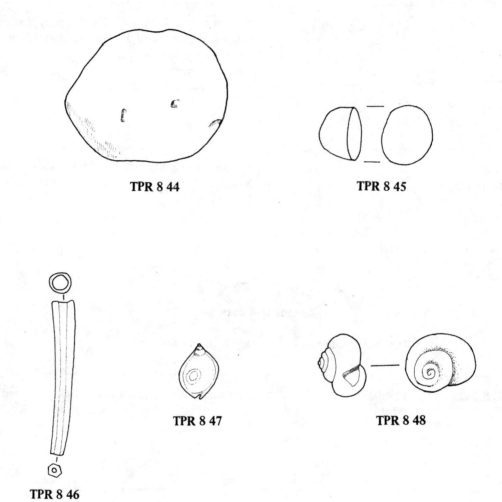

TPR 8 44   TPR 8 45

TPR 8 46   TPR 8 47   TPR 8 48

Figure 18

Designation and Documentation	Dimensions and Stratigraphy	Description and Date
TPR 8 49 Drilled Shell TQ3-134 DeZ-1547	L: 0.9 W: 0.9 Th: 0.7 SG 10, Locus 9, Level 4	*Conus (Lautoconus) mediterraneus* Bruguiere. Modified shell bead. Polished surface. Ends of shell ground. Khana period.
TPR 8 50 Drilled Shell TQ3-335 DeZ-1748	L: 94 W: 1.73 H: 1.04 SG 19, STC A1, FT 22, Locus 4, Level 10	Snail shell with oval perforation. Khana period.
TPR 8 51 Drilled Shell TQ3-291 DeZ-1704 Fig. 19 Ill. 32	L: 5.9 W: 5.5 H: 1.6 SG 11, Level 5	*Spondylus gaedaropus* Linnaeus. Half of bivalve with perforation near hinge. Exterior bright orange. Highly polished near hinge, rest is dull with natural ridges. Mediterranean origin. Mid-third millennium.
TPR 8 52 Drilled Shell TQ3-250 DeZ-1663 Fig. 19	L: 6.5 W: 4.4 H: 1.7 SG 8, FT 3, Level 3	Half of a freshwater clam, *Unio requienii* (?) Linnaeus. Three drilled holes on top. Khana period.
TPR 8 53 Drilled Shell TQ3-111 DeZ-1524 Fig. 19 Ill. 32	L: 4.5 W: 2.2 H: 0.85 SG 6, Locus 2, Level 4	Half of a freshwater clam, *Unio requienii* (?) Linnaeus. Perforation near hinge. Khana period.
TPR 8 54 Drilled Shell TQ3-143 DeZ-1556	L: 0.9 W: 0.7 H: 0.52 SG 9, Locus 4, Level 5	Snail shell. Smooth, shiny, brown exterior. Small perforation at one end. Khana period.

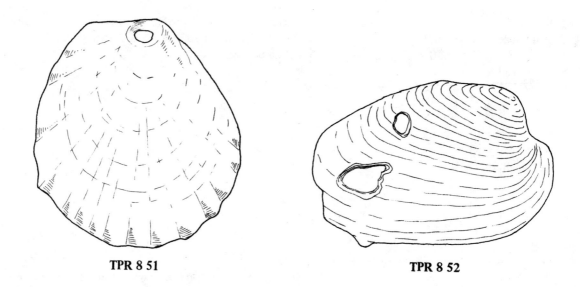

TPR 8 51   **TPR 8 52**

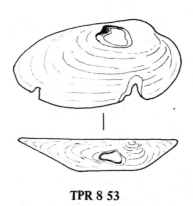

TPR 8 53

Figure 19

Designation and Documentation	Dimensions and Stratigraphy	Description and Date
TPR 8 55 Drilled Shell TQ3-116 DeZ-1529 Fig. 20 Ill. 32	H: 2.1 W: 2.2 Th: 0.8 SG 6, Locus 2, Level 4	*Acanthocardia rustica* Linnaeus. Small perforation near hinge. Mediterranean origin. Khana period.
TPR 8 56 Shell pendant/disc TQ3-156 DeZ-1569 Fig. 20 Ill. 33 AVM DS 2 93	D: 4.2 Th: 0.5 SG 14, Locus 1, Burial 1, Level 7	Incised, polished irridescent shell disc. Top curved; bottom flat. Decorated with three groups of incised circles. Pearly white, powdery surface. Centrally drilled. Bevelled edges. Mid-third millennium.

Comparative Material

Mari: Parrot 1958, Pl. XXIII: No. 1; Fig 19, Fragment B, Court 106;
               1959, Pl. XXVIII: No. 1507, Room 112; Fig. 54:1507 (second millennium)

TPR 8 57 Stone Bead TQ3-176 DeZ-1588 Fig. 20 Ill. 34	L: 1.84 W: 1.77 Th: 0.76 SG 14, Locus 1, Burial 1, Level 7	Diamond-shaped, flat, yellow-orange stone with dull surface. Bevelled corners. Perforated ends flattened. Drilled from both ends along long axis. Mid-third millennium.

Comparative Material

Tell Brak: Mallowan 1947, Pl. XXXIII:22

Tell Chuēra: Moortgat 1965, Pg. 44, Abb. 31

Kish: Mackay 1925, Vol. I, Pl. VII:9 and 11

Mari: Parrot 1956, Pl. LXI, Fig. b
                1962, Pl. XI and XII

Terqa: Thureau-Dangin and Dhorme 1924, Pl. LX, Fig. 4

Ur: Woolley 1934, Pl. 143:d

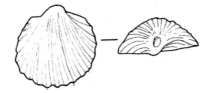

TPR 8 55

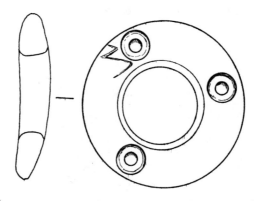

TPR 8 56

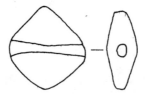

TPR 8 57

Figure 20

Designation and Documentation	Dimensions and Stratigraphy	Description and Date
TPR 8 58 Stone Bead TQ3-168 DeZ-1581 Fig. 21 Ill. 35	L: 2.5 W: 2.1 Th: 0.84 SG 14, Locus 1, Burial 1, Level 7	Diamond-shaped flat, pale orange stone. Perforation along long axis. Perforated ends flattened. Rounded corners. Smooth, dull surface. Drilled from both ends. Mid-third millennium.
TPR 8 59 Stone Bead TQ3-51 DeZ-1464 Fig. 21	H: 0.8 D: 0.87 SG 6, Locus 1, Level 3	Pale to dark amber color. Translucent. Smooth, shiny ground stone. Pitted surface. Round. Khana period.
TPR 8 60 Stone Bead TQ3-49 DeZ-1462 Fig. 21	H: 0.7 D: 0.7 SG 9, Locus 3, Level 3	Amber colored bead. Polished. Pitted surface near perforation. Perforation wider at one end. Khana period.
TPR 8 61 Stone Bead TQ3-133 DeZ-1546 Fig. 21	L: 0.8 W: 0.63 Th: 0.47 SG 14, Locus 1 Level 6	Bright blue. Symmetrical. Flat, rectangular shape with faceted sides. Polished. Central perforation along long axis. Mid-third millennium.
TPR 8 62 Stone Bead TQ3-140 DeZ-1553 Fig. 21	H: 1.9 W: 1.63 Th: 0.7 SG 11, Level 2	Pale green. Translucent. Flat. Bevelled edges. Dull surface. Fragmented. Possibly mid-third millennium.
TPR 8 63 Stone Bead TQ3-162 DeZ-1575 Fig. 21	H: 1.7 W: 1.17 Th: 1.77 SG 9, Locus 3, Level 6	Brown, hollow bead. Shiny surface. Oval perforation. Khana period.
TPR 8 64 Stone Bead TQ3-246 DeZ-1658-9 Fig. 21	L: 2.2 W: 1.4 Th: 0.7 SG 6, FT 22, Level 9	Crude, flat bead with perforation at top. Light grey stone with dull porous surface. Rounded edges. Rectangular shape. Khana period.

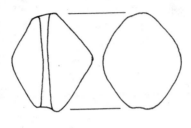

TPR 8 58

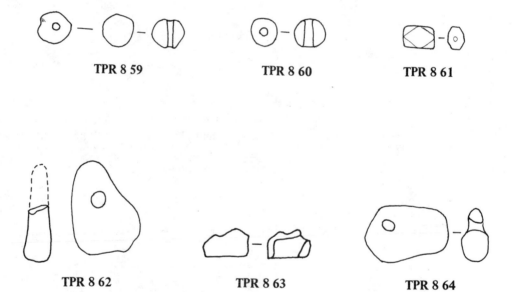

TPR 8 59   **TPR 8 60**   **TPR 8 61**

TPR 8 62   **TPR 8 63**   **TPR 8 64**

Figure 21

Designation and Documentation	Dimensions and Stratigraphy	Description and Date
TPR 8 65 Stone Bead TQ3-256 DeZ-1669 Fig. 22	L: 0.7 H: 0.47 W: 0.42 SG 18, FT 4, Locus 4, Level 7	Tubular. Bright blue. Not perfectly round. Round central perforation along long axis. Dull, smooth surface. Khana period.
TPR 8 66 Stone Bead TQ3-261 DeZ-1674 Fig. 22	H: 0.3 D: 0.55 SG 7, FT 22, Locus 24, Level 8	Round and flat. Translucent orange stone. Central, bevelled perforation. Slightly pitted surface. Smoothed and polished. Khana period.
TPR 8 67 Stone Bead TQ3-132 DeZ-1545 Fig. 22	L: 0.27 D: 0.38 SG 9, Locus 9, Level 4	Oval, blue stone with dull surface. Khana period.
TPR 8 68 Beads TQ3-367 DeZ-1780 Fig. 22	L: 0.7 D: 0.5 SG 19, STC A1, FT 29, Locus 4, Level 11	Two soft white barrel-shaped beads. Dull, pitted surface. Khana period.
TPR 8 69 Stone Bead TQ3-112 DeZ-1525 Fig. 22	L: 1.9 W: 1.0 Th: 0.55 SG 9, Locus 2, Level 4	Brown. Irregular shape. Irregular perforation at one end. Pitted, shiny surface. Khana period.
TPR 8 70 Stone Bead TQ 3-113 DeZ-1526 Fig. 22	H: 1.04 D: 1.0 SG 9, Locus 2, Level 4	Faceted. Green. Square, flattened ends. Polished surface. Khana period.

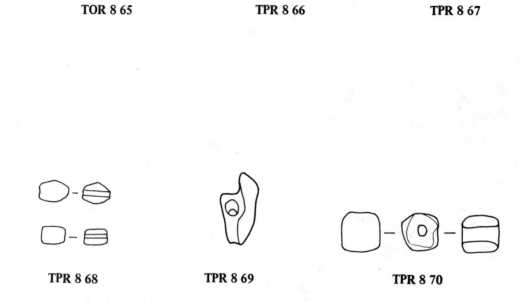

TOR 8 65   TPR 8 66   TPR 8 67

TPR 8 68   TPR 8 69   TPR 8 70

Figure 22

Designation and Documentation	Dimensions and Stratigraphy	Description and Date
TPR 8 71 Stone Bead TQ3-42 DeZ-1455 Fig. 23	H: 0.81 D: 0.85 SG 9, Locus 4, Level 2	Amber color. Flattened ends. Central perforation wider at one end. Smooth surface. Date unknown.
TPR 8 72 Stone Bead. TQ3-110 DeZ-1523 Fig. 23	L: 1.3 D: 0.7 Th: 0.2 SG 9, Locus 2, Level 3	Tubular. Yellow opaque substance (stone?). Dull surface. Slight indentation around perimeter at one end. Khana period.
TPR 8 73 Gypsum Bead TQ3-128 DeZ-1541 Fig. 23 Ill. 36 AVM DS 2 96	H: 1.1 D: 1.7 SG 14, Locus 1, Burial 1, Level 7	Round. White gypsum core covered with shiny white fragments of unidentified substance (quartz?). Associated with the two diamond shaped beads TPR 8 57 and 58 above. Mid-third millennium.
TPR 8 74 Gypsum Beads TQ3-171, 172 and 377 DeZ-1584 and 1790 Fig. 23 Ill. 37 AVM DS 2 98	H: 0.3-0.3 Th: 0.3-0.4 SG 14, Locus 1, Burial 1, Level 7	Round, flat beads. One hundred and sixty beads and eleven fragments found near neck, pelvis, and knees. Beads vary in thickness and diameter. Central perforations. Mid-third millennium.

Comparative Material

Ur: Woolley 1934, Vol. II Text Pg. 87 (reference to beaded girdle)

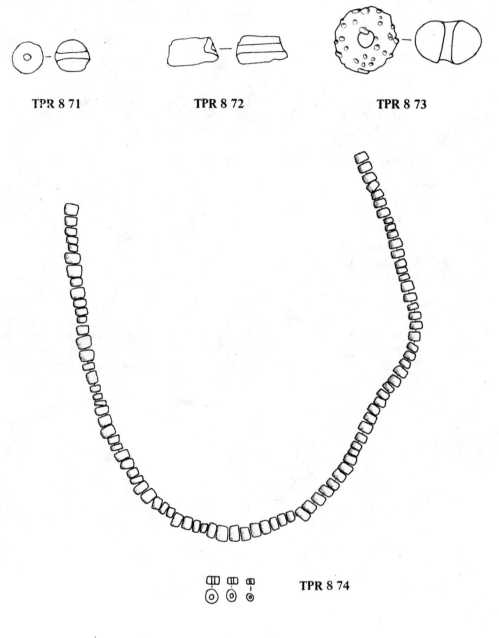

TPR 8 71   TPR 8 72   TPR 8 73

TPR 8 74

Figure 23

Designation and Documentation	Dimensions and Stratigraphy	Description and Date
TPR 8 75 Gypsum Bead TQ3-338 DeZ-1751 Fig. 24	D: 0.9 Th: 0.38 SG 14, Locus 1, Level 7	Round, flat bead. Central perforation round and slanted. Mid-third millennium.
TPR 8 76 Gypsum Bead? TQ3-432 DeZ-1845 Fig. 24	D: 0.75 Th: 0.4 SG 18, Locus 9, FT 32, Level 13 STC A2	Flat, cylindrical bead. Possibly frit. Flattened ends, rounded edges. Central perforation. Rough, dull surface. Khana period.
TPR 8 77 Gypsum Bead TQ3-249 DeZ-1662 Fig. 24	H: 0.65 D: 0.94 SG 6, FT 22, Locus 4, Level 9. On floor.	Round. Central perforation along short axis. Porous, white surface. Khana period.

TPR 8 78
Gypsum Beads?
 	
TQ3-169
DeZ-1582
Fig. 24
	a) L: 0.88 c) H: 0.5
	   D: 0.5 D: 0.6
	
	b) H: 0.38
	   D: 0.8
	
	SG 14, Locus 1,
	Burial 1, Level 7
		One long barrel-shaped bead and two short round beads of a dark, soft, dull unknown composition (gypsum? bitumen? frit?). Identical to TPR 8 86. Traces of white substance on surface. Barrel-shaped bead perforated along long axis. Short, round beads perforated centrally. Mid-third millennium.

TPR 8 79 Gypsum Bead TQ3-158 DeZ-1571 Fig. 24	D: 0.63 Th: 0.42 SG 10, Locus 19, Level 5	Round, flat white bead. Central perforation. Weathered surface. Khana period.
TPR 8 80 Shell or Bone Bead TQ3-161 DeZ-1574 Fig. 24	D: 0.6 Th: 0.14 SG 9, Locus 7, Level 7	Round flat, centrally pierced bead. Dark brown, shiny surface. Khana period.

TPR 8 81
Frit? Beads
 	
TQ3-167
DeZ-1580
Fig. 24
	a) L: 0.05 c) L: 0.54
	   D: 0.55 D: 0.7
	
	b) L: 1.1
	   D: 0.55
	
	SG 14, Locus 1,
	Burial 1, Level 7
		Identical to beads found in container TPR 8 86. Found on and near skull. White substance on surface. One round bead, two oval beads. Long beads perforated along long axis. Round bead centrally perforated. Mid-third millennium.

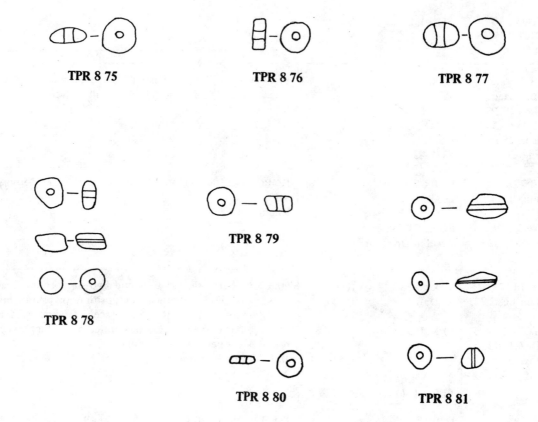

Figure 24

Designation and Documentation	Dimensions and Stratigraphy	Description and Date
TPR 8 82 Bone Bead TQ3-404 DeZ-1817 Fig. 25	H: 0.96 W: 0.9 Th: 0.2 SG 19, STC A1, FT 31, Locus 4, Level 11	Flat and circular. Perforation off-center. Edges of perforation bevelled, polished, and slightly curved. Perforation drilled from both sides. One side smooth and polished, other side dull. Khana period.
TPR 8 83 Frit? Bead TQ3-64 DeZ-1477	L: 1.13 H: 0.34 W: 0.79 SG 9, Locus 3, Level 3	Flat long medium blue bead with three tubular, parallel holes. One side flat, one side ribbed. Incised lines between tubular holes. Dull surface. Khana period.

Comparative Material

Nuzi:	Starr 1937, Pl. 130:E	

Designation and Documentation	Dimensions and Stratigraphy	Description and Date
TPR 8 84 Bitumen Bead? TRQ3-349 DeZ-1762 Fig. 25	L: 0.87 D: 0.8 SG 14, Burial 1, Level 7	Flat, diamond shaped. Soft brown material, possibly frit or bitumen. Mid-third millennium.
TPR 8 85 Glazed Fly Pendant TQ3-375 DeZ-1504 Fig. 25 Ill. 38	L: 2.7 Th: 0.97 SG 7, FT 25, Locus 28, Level 12	Blue glazed fly pendant. Badly weathered. Composition. Khana period?

Comparative Material

Nippur:	McCown et al., Pl. 150:46 (Ur III) and 47 (Assyrian).	
Nuzi:	Starr 1937, Pl. 120:VV	

Designation and Documentation	Dimensions and Stratigraphy	Description and Date
TPR 8 86 Gypsum Container With beads TQ3-166 DeZ-1579 Fig. 25 Ill. 39	L: 4.85 W: 4.1 H: 1.7 SG 14, Locus 1, Burial 1, Level 7	Irregular container with seven beads impressed into surface (only six shown) in Fig. 25. Four beads are barrel shaped, dull, bitumous and porous, of unknown composition; three beads are round and of the same composition. Other bead impressions visible. Mid-third millennium.
TPR 8 87 Haematite Weight TQ3-183 DeZ-1595 Fig. 25 Ill. 40	L: 2.85 W: 1.26 H: 1.18 SG 10, Locus 19, Level 5	Highly polished. Barrel-shaped. Flattened, bevelled ends. Curved. Small nicks on ends. One side slightly flattened. Khana period.

Comparative Material

Terqa:	TPR 3 15	

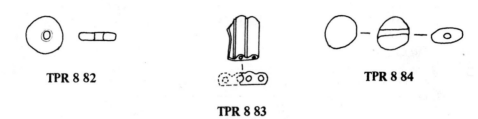

TPR 8 82   **TPR 8 84**

TPR 8 83

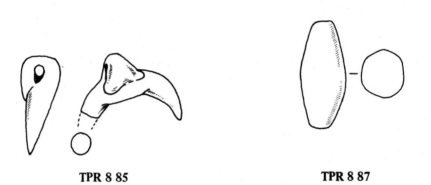

TPR 8 85   **TPR 8 87**

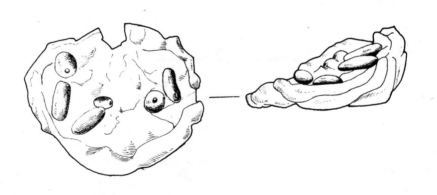

TPR 8 86

Figure 25

Designation and Documentation	Dimensions and Stratigraphy	Description and Date
TPR 8 88 Awl TQ3-115 DeZ-1528 Fig. 26 Ill. 41	L: 11.5 D: 0.5 SG 9, Locus 1, Level 3	Rounded, polished bone. Round perforation. Broken tip, smoothed and reused in antiquity. Khana period.
TPR 8 89 Awl TQ3-196 DeZ-1608 Fig. 26	L: 3.87 D: 0.75 SG 8, STC D2, Level 8	Rounded, polished bone. Round perforation at wide end. Khana period.
TPR 8 90 Awl TQ3-386 DeZ-1799 Fig. 26	L: 3.8 D: 0.5 SG 18, STC A2 FT 23, Locus 7, Level 13	Round, slightly curved bone. Fine abrasions visible on surface. Cracked and brittle with no polish left. Khana period.
TPR 8 91 Awl TQ3-363 DeZ-1776 Fig. 26	L: 3.36 D: 0.53 SG 18, STC A2, Locus 7, Levels 8-9	Tapering central section of bone, round in cross-section. Polished surface. Khana period.
TPR 8 92 Awl TQ3-344 DeZ-1757	L: 8.4 D: 0.69 SG 18, Locus 5, Level 11	Perforated, flattened bone, broken at perforation. Rounded sides. Tapers to a point. Tip broken. Polished surface. Surface abrasions visible. Khana period. ——— Comparative Material Terqa: TPR 3 27
TPR 8 93 Awl TQ3-350 DeZ-1763 Fig. 26	L: 4.2 D: 0.93 SG 18, STC A2 Locus 7, Levels 8-9	Polished, flattened bone with round perforation at wide end. Perforation has bevelled edges. Khana period.

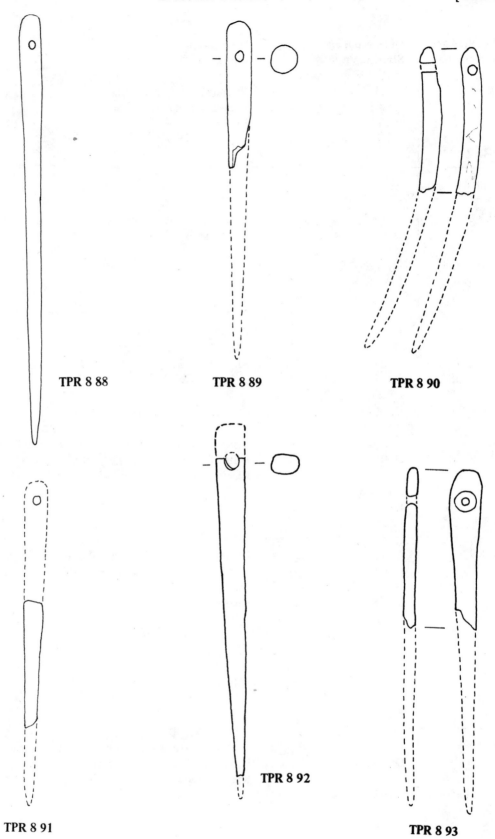

TPR 8 88

TPR 8 89

TPR 8 90

TPR 8 91

TPR 8 92

TPR 8 93

Figure 26

Designation and Documentation	Dimensions and Stratigraphy	Description and Date
TPR 8 94 Ring TQ3-231 DeZ-1643 Fig. 27	D: 2.2 Th: 0.4 SG 14, Locus 3, Level 6	Smoothed and polished bone. Oval in cross-section. Mid-third millennium.
TPR 8 95 Hollow tube TQ3-20 DeZ-1433 Fig. 27	L: 9.12 D: 1.1 SG 10, Level 1	Highly polished bone tube. Bevelled edges. Hollow, smooth interior. Surface abrasions apparent.
TPR 8 96 Unidentified Object TQ3-87 DeZ-1500 Fig. 27 Ill. 42	L: 8.8 D: 1.35 Th: 1.0 W of shaft: 0.6 SG 8, Level 4, Locus 16	Worked bone. Rectangular shaft with flattened, shovel shaped blade. Shaft has two decorated sides and one central perforation. Decoration consists of four sets of incised, concentric circles. Each set has two incised concentric circles with a central depression. One side of shovel shaped blade has one set of concentric circles. Shaft has three sets. Other side has four sets on the shaft. Irregular surface, not perfectly shaped or smoothed. Surface abrasions visible where carved. Khana period.

TPR 8 94

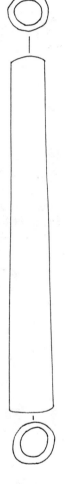

TPR 8 96

TPR 8 95

Figure 27

4. References

BARRELET, MARIE THÉRÈSE
    1968   *Figurines et Reliefs en Terre Cuite de la Mesopotamie Antique,* Vol. I Paris.

BUCCELLATI, G. and M. KELLY-BUCCELLATI
    1978   "Terqa Preliminary Reports 6—The Third Season; Introduction and the Stratigraphic Record," *Syro-Mesopotamian Studies* 2/6:115-164.

du BUISSON, M.
    1932   "Une campagne de fouilles à Khan Sheikhoun," *Syria.* 13 pt. 2:171-88.

FUGMANN, E.
    1958   *Hama, Fouilles et Recherches* 1931-1938. Vol. II 1. Copenhagen.

HALLER, ARNDT
    1954   *Die Gräber und Grüfte von Assur.* Berlin.

HEINRICH, ERNST
    1936   *Kleinfunde aus den archaischen Tempelschichten in Uruk.* Berlin.

KELLY-BUCCELLATI, M. and L. MOUNT-WILLIAMS
    1977   "Terqa Preliminary Reports 3—Object Typology of the Second Season: The Third and Second Millennia," *Syro-Mesopotamian Studies* 1/5:143-169.

KELLY-BUCCELLATI, M. and W. SHELBY
    1977   "Terqa Preliminary Reports 4—A Typology of Ceramic Vessels of the Third and Second Millennia from the First Two Seasons", *Syro-Mesopotamian Studies* 1/6:171-236.

LANGDON, S.
    1924   *Excavations at Kish*, Vol. I. Paris.

    1934   *Excavations at Kish*, Vol. IV. Paris.

LEGRAIN, LEON
    1930   *Terra-cotta from Nippur.* Philadelphia.

MACKAY, E.
    1925   *Report on the Excavation of the "A" Cemetery at Kish, Mesopotamia*, 2 Vols. Berlin.

MAHMOUD, A.
    1978   "Terqa Preliminary Reports 5—Die Industrie der islamischen Keramik aus der zweiten Season", *Syro-Mesopotamian Studies* 2/5:95-114.

MALLOWAN, M.

1937   "The Excavations at Tell Chagar Bazar", *Iraq* IV:91-177.

1947   "Excavations at Brak and Chagar Bazar", *Iraq* IX:1-259.

MCCOWN, D., R. HAINES and D. P. HANSEN
1967   *Nippur* Vol. I. Chicago.

MOORTGAT, ANTON
1960a   *Tell Chuēra in Nordost-Syrien. Vorläufiger Bericht über die Grabung 1958.* Köln und Opladen.

1960b   *Tell Chuēra in Nordost-Syrien. Vorläufiger Bericht über die zweite Grabungskampagne 1969.* Wiesbaden.

1962   *Tell Chuēra in Nordost-Syrien. Vorläufiger Bericht über die dritte Grabungskampagne 1963.* Köln und Opladen.

1965   *Tell Chuēra in Nordost-Syrien. Vorläufiger Bericht über die vierte Grabungskampagne 1963.* Köln und Opladen.

MOORTGAT, ANTON and U. MOORTGAT-CORRENS
1976   *Tell Chuēra in Nordost-Syrien. Vorläufiger Bericht über die siebente Grabungskampagne 1974.* Berlin.

PARROT, ANDRE
1935   "Les fouilles de Mari. Première Campagne (Hiver 1933-1934)", *Syria*, Vol. 16 pt. 1:1-28.

1956   *Le Temple d'Ishtar. Mission Archeologique de Mari*, Vol. I. Paris.

1958   *Le Palais (peintures murales). Mission Archaeologique de Mari*, Vol. II. Paris.

1959   *Le Palais: Documents et Monuments. Mission Archeologique de Mari*, Vol. II. Paris.

1962   "Les Fouilles de Mari. Douzieme Campagne (Automne 1961)", *Syria* 39:151-79.

POWELL, MARVIN
       "A Contribution to the History of Money in Mesopotamia Prior to the Invention of Coinage", forthcoming in Matouš festschrift.

PRAG, KAY
1970   "The 1959 Deep Sounding at Harran in Turkey", *Levant*, Vol. II:63-94.

SCHMANDT-BESSERAT
1977   "An Archaic Recording System and the Origin of Writing", *Syro-Mesopotamian Studies*, Vol. 1/2, pp. 31-70.

SHELBY, W. and E. GRIFFIN
	"Terqa Preliminary Reports 9–Ceramic Vessel Typology of the Third Season",
	Syro-Mesopotamian Studies, in press.

SPEISER, E.
	1935	*Excavations at Tepe Gawra*, Vol. I. Philadelphia.

STARR, RICHARD
	1937	*Nuzi*, Vol. II. Cambridge.

STROMMENGER, E.
	1974	*5000 Years of the Art of Mesopotamia.* New York.

THUREAU-DANGIN, F. and R. P. DHORME
	1924	"Cinq Jours de Fouilles à Asharah", *Syria* 5 pt. 4:34-293.

THUREAU-DANGIN, F. and M. M. DUNAND
	1936	*Til-Barsib.* Paris.

TOUEIR, KASSIM
	1978	"The Sumerian Archaeological Expedition to Tell Al'Abd Zrejehey: Clay
		Figurines of the Third Millennium", *Syro-Mesopotamian Studies*, Vol. 2/4:59-93.

van LOON, M.
	1968	"First Results of the 1967 Excavations at Tell Selenkahiye", *Annales Archeo-
		logiques arabes Syriennes*, Vol. XVIII, 1-2:21-36.

	1973	"A-First Results of the 1972 Excavations at Tell Selenkahiye", *Annales Archeo-
		logiques arabes Syriennes*, Vol. XXIII:145-58.

WOOLEY, LEONARD
	1955	*Alalakh*, London.

	1934	*Ur Excavations, The Royal Cemetery*, Vol. II Text and Plates, London.

WOOLEY, LEONARD and MAX MALLOWAN
	1976	*Ur Excavations, The Old Babylonian Period*, Vol. VII. London.

ZEIGLER, C.
	1962	*Die Terrakotten von Warka*, Berlin.

Volumes of the *Terqa Preliminary Reports* are referred to using the abbreviation *TPR*,
as follows:

	TPR 3:	see Kelly-Buccellati and Mount-Williams 1977
	TPR 4:	see Kelly-Buccellati and Shelby 1977
	TPR 5:	see Mahmoud 1978
	TPR 6:	see Buccellati and Kelly-Buccellati 1978
	TPR 9:	see Shelby and Griffin, in press

Index of Field (Register) Numbers

Abbreviations

A. Documentary

ARTANES   Aids and Research Tools in Near Eastern Studies, Malibu.

TQ3-   Prefix of field registration number for artifacts excavated during the third season at Terqa (Ashara).

AVM DS   Audio-Visual Modules Documentary Series

DeZ-   Prefix of inventory numbers for the Museum of Antiquities, Deir ez-Zor

TPR   Terqa Preliminary Reports

B. Stratigraphic

FT   Feature

SF   Surface find

SG   Sounding (see TPR 6, fig. 1 for location of various operations)

ST   Structure

CF   Chance find